Nita Mehta's
The art of BAKING

NITA MEHTA
B.Sc. (Home Science), M.Sc. (Food & Nutrition) Gold Medalist

Publishers Pvt. Ltd
3A/3 Asaf Ali Road, New Delhi - 110 002
Tel : 3250091, 3252948; Telefax : 6235218

NITA MEHTA'S The art of BAKING

© Copyright 1996-98 Publishers

World Right reserved with the publishers: No portion of this book shall be reproduced, stored in a retrieval system, or transmitted by any means, electronic, mechanical, photocopying, recording or otherwise, without the written permission of the publishers.

Disclaimer: While every precaution has been taken in the preparation of this book, the publisher and the author assume no responsibility for errors or omissions. Neither is any liability assumed for damages resulting from the use of the information contained herein.

Trademarks Acknowledged. Trademarks used, if any, are acknowledged as trademarks of their respective owners. These are used as reference only and no trademark infringement is intended upon.

First Edition 1996, Fourth Reprint 1998
ISBN 81-86004-13-0

Layout and laser typesetting:

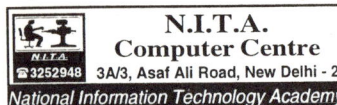

Published by:

Publishers Pvt Ltd, 3A/3 Asaf Ali Road, New Delhi-110002
Editorial & Marketing office: **E-348, Greater Kailash-II, N.Delhi-48**
Fax: 6235218 Phone: 6238727, 3250091, 3252948, 6214011
E-Mail: 1. snab@snabindia.com; 2. sppl.snab@axcess.net.in
Website: http://www.snabindia.com

Distributed by:
THE VARIETY BOOK DEPOT
A.V.G. Bhavan, M 3 Con Circus,
New Delhi - 110 001
Tel: 3327175, 3322567; Fax: 3714335

Printed at:
NUTECH PHOTOLITHOGRAPHERS
4759/XI, Pratap Street,
23, Daryaganj, New Delhi - 110 002.
Tel: 3268423, 3273693; Fax: 91-11-3262241

Contents

MEAL TIME DISHES - CONTINENTAL TASTE 11
- Vegetable Au Gratin 12
- Macaroni-Cheese 14
- Grantinated Cabbage 16
- Cauliflower & Mushroom Bake 20
- Baby Corn & Leafy Spinach 22
- Cheesy Noodles 24
- Hot Cheese Souffle 27
- Cauliflower Noisette 28

MEAL TIME DISHES - INDIAN TASTE 29
- Stuffed Capsicum 30

Potato Surprise 32
Tomato Cups 33
Beans & Macaroni Delight 34
Spinach Cheese Medley 38
Grantinated Vegatable Lasagna 41
Beans in Potato Nest 44
Vegetable Cannelloni 46
Baked Cauliflower 50
Quick Casserole 52
Baked Spinach with Noodles 56

SWEET TEA -TIME EATS 59
Pin Wheel Biscuits 60
Short Crust Pastry (Basic Recipe) 62

Cinnamon Apple Pie   64
Jam Tarts   66
Choux Pastry (Basic Recipe)   67
Chocolate Eclairs   68
Nut & Date Cubes   70
Malai Biscuits   74
Eggless Victorian Cake   75
Madeleines   76
Peanut Macaroons   78
Coconut Macaroons   79
Cashewnut Cookies   80

SAVOURY TEA-TIME EATS   81

Savoury Mushroom Loaf   82
Special Crusty Pizza   84

Cheese Straws 87
Paneer Potato Ring 88
Pleated Bread 90
Cheese on Toast 92

BAKED RICE, ROTIS & BREAD ROLLS 93

Crispy Baked Biryani 94
Bread Rolls 96
Moulded Spanish Rice 98
Tandoori Parantha 100
Mexican Rice Casserole 102

Which oven should I buy?

I have been asked this question several times during my cookery classes. May be, you too have the same question in mind.

Ovens generally fall into two categories -

The round ones costing around Rs.500. If you want to buy this, keep in mind that you should buy the largest size and the oven should have a thermostat attached which can control the oven's temperature. If you already possess a round oven without the temperature control, you could ask any electrical shop to get it fixed for you on your oven.

The other oven is a square (rectangular) one which costs around Rs. 2,500-3000. Again, remember to buy a big size, so that your big baking tins & dishes can go into it. The space in between, I mean the height of the oven should be enough. If it is less, your food may get burnt because it is going to be placed very near to the heating coils which are at the top & bottom of the oven.

Out of the two ovens you could choose any one which suits your pocket. The square one (expensive one) bakes a little faster than the round one because it has two coils where as the round one has only one coil at the bottom. Browning may be slower in the round one.

But which ever oven you have, the final product does not depend on the price of the oven. It depends on your effort to understand your oven & the practice you do with your oven. So read further....

Understand your oven.......

For perfect results, it is important to understand your oven.

If you have a square oven....

The square oven has two coils, one at the top & the other at the bottom. Normally we keep both the coils on, when we bake, but if your biscuits or any other dish gets extra brown too early, you may switch off the upper coil. Bake with one coil on only, so that the inside of your food gets cooked, but if in the end you feel it is taking too long to cook fully, you could switch on your top coil again for a few minutes. Let me explain to you in a simpler way. When you cook a vegetable, say Aloo-Gobi, you bhuno it on high flame, (the same as having both coils on) then slow down the flame (switching off the upper coil & leaving the bottom coil burning) & in the end for a few minutes if you cook on high flame again, the look of your vegetable turns out better. Apply the same to your oven if it troubles you while baking. Normally if the temperature is right & the voltage is right, dishes get baked properly without having to tamper with the knobs.

In the round ovens there is just one coil & you cannot do much with it. Although, it takes a little more time than the square oven, it gives you a perfect baked product, making the saying true - " slow & steady wins the race!"

Oven Temperature Chart

°C	°F	Gas Mark	
110	225	¼	Very slow
130	250	½	
140	275	1	Slow
150	300	2	
170	325	3	
180	350	4	
190	375	5	
200	400	6	Fairly hot
220	425	7	
230	450	8	Hot
240	475	9	Very hot

MEAL TIME
dishes for the
CONTINENTAL TASTE

» Vegetable au Gratin «

Serves 8

WHITE SAUCE
4 tbsp butter
4 tbsp maida (plain flour)
3 cups milk
salt, pepper to taste
1 tbsp tomato ketchup

VEGETABLES
10-15 french beans - cut diagonally into small pieces
2 carrots - cut into small cubes
½ small cauliflower - cut into small flowerettes
½ cup shelled peas
1 medium potato - cut into small cubes
½ small (250 gms) ghiya (bottle gourd) - cut into small cubes

TOPPING
¼ cup bread crumbs
1 firm tomato - sliced

1. To prepare the sauce, heat butter in a clean heavy bottomed pan, on low flame.
2. When butter melts, add the flour & mix stirring continuously on low flame for 1 minute. Do not let the colour change.
3. Remove from fire & add milk. Mix well. Return to fire & stir continuously till the sauce becomes thick.
4. Add salt, pepper and tomato ketchup to it. Keep sauce aside.
5. Wash vegetables & pressure cook with 1 tsp salt with ¼ cup water, till the hissing sound starts. Remove from fire before the whistle. Strain vegetables. Cool.
6. Mix steamed vegetables with the prepared sauce. Add salt if required.
7. Transfer to a shallow borosil dish. Arrange tomato slices over it. Sprinkle bread crumbs. Bake in a hot oven at 240°C/475°F, till golden brown for about 35 minutes. Remove from the oven & serve hot.

» Macaroni-Cheese «

Serves 4

3/4 cup (50 gm) macaroni - boiled
2½ tbsp butter
1 bread slice - sides removed & crumbled to form crumbs
½ small onion - very finely chopped
2 t bsp maida (flour)
1½ cups milk
½ tsp salt
¼ tsp mustard powder
½ tsp pepper
25 gm cheese - grated

GARNISHING
coriander, parsley or mint

1. Boil 4- cups water with 1 tsp salt & 1 tsp oil. Add macaroni to boiling water. Cook for 8-10 minutes till tender. Remove from fire & leave in hot water for 7-8 minutes. Strain. Put in cold water for 2-3 minutes. Strain again. Keep aside.
2. Melt ½ tbsp butter in a small saucepan over medium heat. Remove from fire & add bread crumbs and toss to coat. Keep aside.
3. For cheese sauce, melt remaining 2 tbsp butter in a saucepan and add finely chopped onion and cook till it turns transparent. Stir in flour, and cook for 1 minute. Slowly add milk, stirring continuously. Cook until smooth & slightly thickened such that it coats the spoon, stirring constantly. Add salt, mustard powder and pepper powder. Remove from heat. Stir in the grated cheese until melted.
4. Place drained macaroni in a baking dish greased with butter. Pour cheese sauce over macaroni. Sprinkle buttered bread crumbs on top.
5. Bake in a hot oven at 220°C/425°F for 15-20 minutes or till bubbly and bread crumbs turn golden brown.
6. Serve hot garnished with parsley or mint.

» Gratinated Cabbage «

Serves 6

1 small sized cabbage - cut into 4 big pieces
1 carrot - cut into round slices
1 tomato - sliced paper thin
¼ tsp dry mustard powder or to taste
50 gm cheese - grated
2 tbsp bread crumbs

WHITE SAUCE
3 tbsp butter
3 tbsp maida (plain flour)
2½ cups milk
3/4 tsp salt, ½ tsp pepper

Cheesy Noodles : Page 24

1. Boil 4-5 cups water with 2 tsp salt. Add carrot. Boil till half cooked. Add the quartered cabbage and cook for about 4-5 minutes, until just tender. Remove from fire. Do not over cook. Drain the vegetables. Cool. Shred cabbage finely into thin long pieces.
2. Place shredded cabbage & carrots in a greased ovenproof dish.
3. Arrange a layer of sliced tomatoes.
4. To prepare the white sauce, melt butter in a heavy bottomed pan. Add maida & cook on low flame for 1-2 minutes. Remove from fire.
5. Add milk, stirring continuously.
6. Return to fire. Cook till thick. Add salt & pepper.
7. Add dry mustard powder.
8. Pour the white sauce over the tomatoes, leaving the edges such that the vegetables look appetizing at the time of serving.
9. Sprinkle with grated cheese and bread crumbs and brown in a preheated oven at 200°C/400°F. Serve at once.

Tomato Cups : Page 33

» Cauliflower & Mushroom Bake «

Serves 4

½ small cauliflower
100 gms mushrooms
2 onions - finely sliced
2 tbsp butter
1 cup (150 gms) cream or ½ cup malai
25 gms cheese

WHITE SAUCE
3 tbsp butter
3 tbsp maida (plain flour)
2½ cups milk
3/4 tsp salt
½ tsp pepper

1. Cut cauliflower into medium flowerettes without stalk.
2. Boil in water with a little salt till just done. Do not over cook.
3. Heat butter & fry onions till brown. Remove from butter & keep aside.
4. Remove stalks from mushrooms. Saute whole mushrooms in butter on slow fire till cooked. Keep aside.
5. To prepare white sauce, melt butter in a heavy bottomed pan. Add maida & cook on slow fire for 1-2 minutes. Remove from fire.
6. Add milk gradually, stirring continuously.
7. Return to fire. Cook till thick. Add salt & pepper. Remove from fire & add cream.
8. To assemble, grease an oven proof dish.
9. Arrange a layer of fried onions, keeping aside a few for the top.
10. Spread boiled cauliflower over it.
11. Spread half of the white sauce over the cauliflower.
12. Arrange mushrooms. Cover with white sauce.
13. Bake at 240°C/475°F for 20-30 minutes till light brown.
14. Sprinkle fried onions. Grate cheese.
15. Bake again for 5-7 minutes. Serve immediately.

» Baby Corn & Leafy Spinach «

Serves 6

8 baby corns - cut into ½" pieces
250 gm spinach (paalak)
1 tbsp butter, 1 tsp oil
1 onion - chopped, 4 flakes garlic - chopped
½ tsp black pepper powder (freshly & coarsely ground), salt to taste
25 gm cheddar cheese or any other brand

WHITE SAUCE
2½ tbsp butter
2½ tbsp maida (plain flour)
1¾ cups milk
½ tsp pepper powder, salt to taste
90 ml/ 6 tbsp cream or thin fresh malai
75 gm cheddar cheese or any other brand

1. To prepare the sauce, melt butter in a saucepan, add flour and cook over very low heat for 1 minute, stirring constantly. Remove from fire.
2. Add milk, stirring constantly. Return to fire & cook until it turns thick.
3. Keeping the flame low, add corn to the prepared sauce. Add pepper and salt.
4. Add the cheese and cream, stir and then simmer, stirring occasionally, for 3 minutes. Adjust the salt. Keep sauce aside.
5. To prepare the spinach, wash & put it in boiling water for 4-5 minutes. Drain, put in iced water, drain, squeeze out the excess water in a strainer or with the hands and chop finely.
6. Heat the butter and oil. Add onions & cook until they turn transparent. Add garlic and cook until golden brown.
7. Add spinach and salt, cook until the liquid has almost evaporated.
8. Evenly spread spinach to make a bed in a casserole dish, pour on the cooked corn pieces along with the sauce. Grate cheddar cheese on top, put in a preheated oven at 180°C/350°F and bake until golden. Serve.

» Cheesy Noodles «

Picture on page 17

Serves 4

BOIL TOGETHER
50 gms (½ packet) chow noodles
1 tsp oil
6 cups water
1 tsp salt

CHEESE SAUCE
4 tbsp butter
4 tbsp maida (plain flour)
2½ cups milk (cold)
1 tsp salt or to taste
½ tsp pepper
25 gms (1 cube)

GARNISHING
½ tomato
½ capsicum
1 cube (25 gm) cheese
1 tsp butter

1. Boil 6 cups water with salt & oil in a large pan.
2. Put ½ packet of noodles into the boiling water. Open noodles with a fork. Boil on high flame for 3 minutes. Remove from fire.
3. Strain the noodles. Add fresh water & strain once again. Keep adding cold water & straining till the noodles are no longer hot.
4. Keep them in the strainer for 10 minutes. Sprinkle 1 tsp oil & gently mix. Keep aside.
5. To prepare the sauce, heat butter on low flame in a clean heavy bottomed pan.
6. When butter melts, add the flour & mix stirring continuously on low flame for 1 minute.

7. Remove from fire & add milk. Mix well. Return to fire & stir continuously till the sauce becomes thick & coats the spoon.
8. Keeping the flame low, add salt & pepper.
9. Grate one cube (25 gms) of cheese & mix with the hot sauce.
10. Mix the boiled noodles with the sauce. Add more salt & pepper if required. Remove from fire.
11. Grease a shallow borosil dish (2" high) & transfer the noodle mix in it.
12. Bake in a preheated oven at 200°C/400°F for ½ hour or till the top turns brown.
13. Remove from oven. Grate a cube of cheese over the baked noodles.
14. Remove pulp of tomato & seeds of capsicum. Cut into very thin ½" long pieces & sprinkle over the grated cheese. Dot with butter at 4-5 places.
15. Put the noodles back into the oven & bake for another 5-7 minutes. Serve hot.

» Hot Cheese Souffle «

Serves 4

2 tbsp flour
2 tbsp butter
150 ml (slightly less than 1 cup) milk
3 eggs
75 gm cheese - grated
salt, pepper & mustard powder to taste

1. Melt the butter and stir in the flour. Stir for 1 minute.
2. Gradually add the milk stirring continuously until smooth. Cook till thick.
3. Remove from fire. Cool slightly. Separate eggs. Add egg yolks to the sauce one by one, beating well. Add cheese, salt, pepper & mustard pd.
4. Beat egg whites stiffly & fold gently into the sauce. Transfer to a greased ovenproof or souffle dish. Bake in a moderately hot oven at 400°F/200°C, for about 20 minutes, till well risen and brown. Serve at once.

» Cauliflower Noisette «

Picture on page 53

Serves 4

1 medium cauliflower - broken into medium flowerettes
100 gm cheddar cheese or any other cheese - grated
salt and pepper
2 tbsp butter - melted
1 tbsp chopped coriander - to garnish (optional)

1. Cook the cauliflower flowerettes in boiling salted water until just tender. Do not over cook. Drain well.
2. Grease an ovenproof dish with some butter and cover the bottom with a layer of grated cheese, using half of it.
3. Spread the cauliflower over it. Sprinkle with salt & pepper.
4. Sprinkle left over cheese. Heat butter until it melts and pour over the cheese. Brown under a grill for 10 min. Garnish with chopped coriander.

MEAL TIME
dishes for the
INDIAN TASTE

» Stuffed Capsicum «

Serves 6

3 large capsicums
a pinch of soda bicarb
a few coriander leaves dipped in chilled water - for garnishing

FILLING
1 onion - finely chopped
2 tbsp oil
6-7 saboot kali mirch (pepper corns) - coarsely powdered
1 green chilli - finely chopped
1 small tomato - finely chopped
1 cup cooked rice or 1 boiled, grated potato
150 gms paneer (cottage cheese) - mashed roughly
½ tsp salt - (to taste), 3/4 tsp chaat masala -(to taste)
2 tsp butter

1. Cut capsicums into halves, lengthwise & scoop out.
2. Boil 5-6 cups water to which 1 tsp salt and a pinch of soda bicarb has been added. Add capsicums to the boiling water.
3. Remove after 1 minute.
4. Keep them upside down for a few minutes.
5. To prepare the filling, heat oil. Add onion & cook till transparent. Add crushed pepper corns. Cook for 1 minute.
6. Add tomato and green chillies. Cook for 2-3 minutes.
7. Add grated boiled potato or rice and roughly mashed paneer. Add salt & chaat masala. Cook for a few minutes. Remove from fire.
8. Mix butter with the hot filling.
9. Put the filling in the scooped capsicum halves. Press. Put a little more filling to heap it in the centre above the level of the capsicum.
10. Place on a greased tray & bake for 8-10 minutes.
11. Do not over bake, serve immediately, garnished with a coriander leaf.

» Potato Surprise «

Picture on page 36

Serves 4

4 really large potatoes
2½ tbsp salted butter
salt & pepper to taste
1 cube (25 gm) cheese - grated
3 tbsp chopped coriander

1. Boil potatoes in their jackets until tender. Cut a ¼" thick slice from the top of the potatoes. Scoop out the pulp with a spoon, leaving a border of ¼" all around. Rub soft butter on the border & inside the potato.
2. Mash the scooped out potatoes gently with a fork. Add 2 tbsp butter, salt, pepper, coriander & grated cheese.
3. Remove skin of potatoes carefully. Pile potato mix into the potato cases. Bake in a hot oven at 240°C/475°F or place under a hot grill to brown.

» Tomato Cups «

Picture on page 18

Serves 6

6 large firm tomatoes
100 gm (½ packet) mushrooms - sliced finely
2 tbsp oil
3/4 cup cooked basmati rice, 2 tsp butter
salt & pepper to taste, mint leaves (poodina) - to garnish

1. Cut a slice from the top of the tomatoes, scoop out and chop the pulp. Keep the tops aside. Rub salt on the inner part of the tomatoes.
2. Fry the mushrooms in oil till they turn brown and get cooked.
3. Add the tomato pulp and fry for 2-3 minutes. Add salt & pepper. Add rice and fry for about 3-4 minutes. Add butter. Mix. Remove from fire.
4. Spoon rice mixture into the tomato cases. Place the tops upright as shown in the picture. Bake in a greased tray, at 375°F/190°C for 10 minutes. Serve at once garnished with mint leaves.

» Beans & Macaroni Delight «

Serves 6

1 cup macaroni - boiled
1 small tin (1 cup) baked beans
2 capsicums - cut into rings
1 onion - cut into rings
3 tomatoes - pureed
1 tsp maida (plain flour)
1" piece ginger - finely grated
½ tsp red chilli powder
½ tsp salt
2 tbsp butter
50 gms cheese
1 tbsp tomato ketchup - optional

Beans in Potato Nest : Page 44

1. Put 3 tomatoes in hot water for 5-7 minutes. Remove skin & puree in a blender. Dissolve 1 tsp maida in it & keep aside.
2. Heat 1½ tbsp butter in a kadhai. Add crushed garlic. Cook for 1 minute. Add onion rings & stir fry till transparent.
3. Add capsicum rings & stir fry for 1-2 minutes. Remove a few onion & capsicum rings from the kadhai & keep aside for garnishing.
4. Add ginger & red chilli powder. Add tomato puree & stir fry for 2-3 minutes till it turns a little dry.
5. Mix baked beans. Stir in the boiled macaroni gently. Add tomato ketchup if you like the sweet taste. Add salt & pepper to taste.
6. Transfer to a greased baking dish.
7. Sprinkle the fried onion & capsicum rings.
8. Grate cheese on it & dot with butter at 3-4 places.
9. Bake in a moderately hot oven at 180°C/350°F for 15-20 minutes.

Potato Surprise : Page 32

» Spinach Cheese Medley «

Serves 8

1 cup finely chopped paalak (spinach)
½ cup (75 gm) paneer (cottage cheese) - grated
2 onions - finely chopped
1 tomato - chopped
½ tsp salt
½ tsp pepper
4-5 flakes garlic - crushed
2 tbsp butter

ALOO & PANEER MASALA
2 potatoes - boiled & grated
150 gms paneer - grated
2 tbsp finely chopped coriander
2 green chillies - chopped finely

juice of one lemon
½ tsp salt
¼ tsp pepper

GARNISHING
4 tbsp grated cheese
1 firm tomato - sliced

1. Prepare the aloo-paneer masala by mixing all the ingredients well. Keep aside.
2. Heat butter & add crushed garlic. Add finely chopped onion. Fry for 2-3 minutes till light brown. Add tomato. Cook for 1-2 minutes.
3. Add chopped spinach and salt. Cook for 4-5 minutes till the spinach gets cooked.
4. Add grated paneer. Mix well. Remove from fire.
5. Grease a borosil baking dish & spread the aloo-paneer masala at the bottom.
6. Spread spinach & paneer over it.

7. Grate cheese over it.
8. Decorate with a row of sliced tomatoes overlapping each other in the centre only & bake in a hot oven at 200°C/400°F for 15 minutes. Serve hot.

» Gratinated Vegetable Lasagna «

Picture on page 72

Serves 7-8

LASAGNA
50 gm (½ cup) paalak (spinach) - chopped
1 cup maida
½ tsp salt, 2 tsp butter

VEGETABLES
1 potato - grated, 1 carrot - grated
½ cup shredded cabbage
¼ cup shredded casicum
½ tsp salt, ¼ tsp pepper
2 tbsp butter
¼ tsp ajwain or a pinch of oregano
4 tbsp (25 gm) cheese - grated

TOMATO SAUCE
250 gm (3 big) tomatoes - chopped roughly
1 tbsp tomato ketchup
¼ tsp red chilli powder, ½ tsp salt, ¼ tsp pepper
1 tbsp butter

WHITE SAUCE
2 tbsp butter
2 tbsp maida (plain flour)
1½ cups milk - cold
¼ tsp black pepper powder, ½ tsp salt

1. Wash & grind paalak to a paste with 1 tbsp water.
2. Sift maida. Rub in butter. Add paalak paste & salt. Knead to a firm dough. Cover & keep aside for 30 minutes.
3. To prepare the vegetables, melt butter. Add ajwain & fry for 1 minute on low flame. Add potatoes. Cook for 2 minutes. Add carrot & cabbage. Add salt & pepper. Toss for a minute. Add cheese. Remove from fire.
4. To prepare the tomato sauce, cook chopped tomatoes in ½ cup water

till soft. Strain or blend in a mixer. Put the tomato puree on fire. Add salt, & red chilli. Add butter & tomato ketchup. Cook for a few minutes on low flame. Remove from fire. Keep aside.

5. To prepare the white sauce melt butter in a heavy bottomed pan. Add maida & stir for 1 minute. Add milk, stirring continuously. Cook till it turns thick. Add salt & pepper.

6. To prepare lasagna, keep a pan with 6-7 cups water and 2 tsp oil & 2 tsp salt on fire.

7. Roll out the ready green dough very thinly (paper thin). Cut into long strips, about ½" wide. Put the strips in boiling water. Boil for 8-10 minutes. Stir with a fork. Remove the ready lasagna from the boiling water & mix with the prepared tomato sauce.

8. To assemble, spread lasagna in a greased baking dish. Spread sauted vegetables. Spread white sauce. Bake in a hot oven till golden brown for 15-20 minutes.

Note : If ready-made lasagna is available, you need not make the effort of preparing lasagna at home. Just boil some ready lasagna noodles in salted water with 1 tsp of oil for 8-10 minutes till soft.

» Beans in Potato Nest «

Picture on page 35

Serves 6

BEANS
1½ cups boiled (with salt) rajmah (kidney beans)
alternately, a tin of baked beans can be used
3 tbsp salted butter
¼ cup tomato ketchup

MASHED POTATOES
6 boiled potatoes - grated
1 tbsp salted butter
2-3 tbsp hot milk
¼ tsp pepper
salt to taste

GARNISHING
25 gms cheese
a few mint leaves - dipped in chilled water for ½ hour

1. To prepare the rajmah, add butter and tomato ketchup to the boiled rajmah and cook on low flame till almost dry. Add salt & pepper to taste.
2. To prepare the mashed potatoes, add all ingredients to the potatoes & mix with a fork.
3. To assemble, grease a shallow oven proof dish. Arrange ½" thick layer of potatoes at the base & sides of the dish to form a ring. Mark with a fork on the sides. Bake till potatoes turn golden. Remove from the oven.
4. Fill the center with prepared rajmah or tinned baked beans. Grate cheese on top. Bake for 5-7 minutes. Garnish with mint leaves. Serve immediately.

Note : If you use a tin of baked beans, do not mix butter and tomato ketchup with the beans. Just dry the beans on fire for 5-7 minutes.

» Vegetable Cannelloni «

Serves 6

DOUGH FOR THE CANNELLONI
1 cup maida (plain flour)
¼ tsp salt
1 tbsp oil

FILLING
20 french beans - chopped finely
1 small carrot - chopped finely
1 potato - chopped finely
½ cup shelled peas
2 onions - chopped finely
½ tsp black pepper
½ tsp red chilli powder
1 $^3/_4$ tsp salt or to taste

2 tbsp tomato ketchup
3 tbsp oil

SAUCE
400 gms (4 big) tomatoes - blanched, skinned and pureed
5 - 6 flakes garlic - crushed - optional
2 tbsp oil
2 onions - finely chopped
1 tsp salt
½ tsp red chilli powder
½ tsp pepper
1 tsp sugar
1 tbsp fresh (poodina) mint - chopped
½ cup cream - lightly whipped or ¼ cup fresh malai

TOPPING
4 tbsp (1 cube - 25 gm) cheese
1 tbsp butter

1. Sift maida with salt. Mix maida & oil with a little water to prepare a firm dough. Knead for 10 minutes till smooth & elastic.
2. To prepare the cannelloni, roll out the pasta dough on a lightly floured board until paper-thin. Cut into 3" x 4" rectangles. Cover & set aside for 1 hour.
3. Boil plenty of water in a large pan with 1-2 tsp oil & salt. Drop 2-3 cannelloni into rapidly boiling salted water, and cook until just tender (about 5 minutes). Stir with a wooden spoon to prevent them from sticking to one another. Remove and drain. Spread on a clean cloth to dry.
4. To prepare the filling, steam the vegetables. Put finely chopped beans, carrots, peas & potatoes along with ¼ cup water in a pressure cooker. Pressure cook till the hissing sound starts. Remove from fire.
5. Heat 3 tbsp oil & add onions. Cook till onions turn light pink.
6. Add the boiled vegetables. Add 1½ tsp salt, pepper, & red chilli powder. Stir fry for 3-4 minutes. Add tomato ketchup. Remove from fire.

7. To prepare the tomato sauce, heat the oil and fry the onions and garlic until soft but not browned. Stir in the tomato puree, mint & sugar. Bring to boil. Reduce the heat and add the cream gradually. Mix in the salt, red chilli powder & pepper to taste. Simmer for 5 minutes. Set aside.
8. Place the filling in the cannelloni and roll up to enclose it. Spread the sauce thinly over the bottom of an ovenproof dish.
9. Arrange the cannelloni, side by side, open ends down, over the sauce. Spread with the remaining sauce. Sprinkle over with grated cheese. Melt 1 tbsp butter & pour over the cheese.
10. Bake uncovered in a preheated oven (400°F/200°C for 20 minutes or until lightly browned on top. Serve hot.

» Baked Cauliflower «

Serves 6

2 very small whole cauliflowers

MASALA
3 onions - sliced finely
3 tomatoes - roughly chopped
1" ginger - chopped
2 tbsp curd, 2-3 tbsp milk
½ tsp gram masala, ½ tsp red chilli powder, ½ tsp amchoor
salt to taste
¼ cup boiled or frozen peas - to garnish

1. Remove stems of cauliflowers. Wash whole cauliflowers.
2. Heat ½ cup water in a pressure cooker. Put both cauliflowers with flower side up. Pressure cook on medium flame till the hissing sound starts. Remove from fire.

3. To prepare masala, grind onions to a paste.
4. Heat ½ tbsp oil in a clean kadhai. Add the chopped tomatoes & ginger. Cook for 4-5 minutes till they turn soft. Grind the cooked tomatoes to a paste. Keep tomato paste aside.
5. Heat 3 tbsp oil in a kadahi. Add the onion paste, cook till onions turn brown.
6. Add tomato paste. Cook for 3-4 minutes on low flame till masala turns dry.
7. Add well beaten curd. Cook till masala turns reddish again.
8. Add red chilli pd., amchoor & garam masala. Add salt to taste. Cook for 1 minute.
9. Add 2-3 tbsp milk to get a thick, dry masala. Boil. Cook for 1 minute on low flame. Remove from fire.
10. Insert a little masala in between the florets of the steamed cauliflower.
11. Arrange the cauliflowers on a baking dish. Pour masala over the arranged cauliflowers. Sprinkle some boiled peas on it & on the sides.
12. Bake in a preheated oven at 180°C/350°F for 10-15 minutes. Serve.

» Quick Casserole «

Serves 4

2 small brinjals (long variety) - sliced
2 potatoes - boiled
1 tomato - sliced thinly
2 tbsp chopped coriander
3 tbsp butter
salt, pepper to taste
oil to fry
50 gm cheese - grated

Cauliflower Noisette : Page 28

1. Slice brinjals into thin rounds. Shallow fry in oil in a pan, till light brown in colour.
2. Boil potatoes carefully. Do not over boil. Peel & slice them. Keep aside.
3. Melt butter in a small pan.
4. Grease a baking dish. Spread half of the brinjals. Sprinkle a little salt & pepper.
5. Spread 2 tbsp grated cheese on the brinjals.
6. Spread half of the potatoes on the cheese. Pour half the melted butter on the potatoes.
7. Arrange a layer with half of the tomatoes. Sprinkle salt & pepper.
8. Repeat the layers using the left over brinjals, then a sprinkling of cheese, & then a layer of tomatoes.
9. Arrange a final layer of potatoes, slightly overlapping each other. Pour melted butter carefully on all the slices. Sprikle some chopped coriander.
10. Bake in a preheated oven at 200°C/400°F till potatoes turn golden.
11. Garnish with freshly chopped coriander.

Savoury Mushroom Loaf : Page 82

» Baked Spinach with Noodles «

Serves 4

250 gm paalak (spinach) - chopped finely
½ " piece ginger
1-2 green chillies
2 pinches soda bicarb
½ tsp salt
½ tsp sugar
50 gms noodles - boiled
1 tbsp bread crumbs

TOMATO SAUCE
150 gm (2 big) tomatoes - grated
½" stick dalchini (cinnamon)
2-3 laung (cloves)
8-10 saboot kali mirch (pepper corns)

2 tbsp tomato ketchup
2 small onions - chopped finely
2 tbsp butter
1 tsp maida

WHITE SAUCE
1½ tbsp butter
1 cup milk
1½ tbsp maida
2 tbsp grated cheese
salt & pepper to taste

1. To prepare the tomato sauce, put tomatoes in boiling water for 10 minutes. Remove skin of the tomatoes. Blend in a blender. Keep tomato puree aside.
2. Grind dalchini, laung & pepper corns together. Keep ground masala aside.
3. Heat oil. Add onions. Cook till transparent.

4. Add maida, stirring continuously.
5. Add tomato puree. Add half of the freshly ground masala & ½ tsp salt. Cook till thick & pulpy. Add tomato ketchup. Keep tomato sauce aside.
6. Pressure cook chopped spinach, ginger, green chillies with ¼ cup water & a pinch of soda bicarb to give 2 whistles.
7. Strain & grind spinach to a puree. Add ¼ tsp salt & sugar. Keep spinach puree on fire & cook till dry.
8. Prepare white sauce by melting butter in a clean heavy bottomed pan.
9. Add maida. Cook, stirring, for 1 minute. Add milk & stir till thick.
10. Add ¼ tsp salt & 2 tbsp grated cheese. Remove from fire.
11. Divide white sauce into two parts. Mix one part with spinach puree & the other half with noodles.
12. To assemble spread a layer of spinach in a greased baking dish.
13. Spread noodles in white sauce over it.
14. Spread tomato sauce over it.
15. Sprinkle bread crumbs & grate cheese over it.
16. Dot with butter. Bake till golden brown.

Sweet
TEA TIME
Eats

» Pin Wheel Biscuits «

Makes 16

240 gm (2½ cups) flour (maida)
½ tsp vanilla essence
1 tsp baking powder
1/8 tsp salt
120 gm (slightly less than 3/4 cup) butter
120 gm (slightly less than 1 cup) powdered sugar
3 tbsp milk
3 tbsp cocoa powder

1. Sieve flour, baking powder and salt together.
2. Cream butter and powdered sugar till light and fluffy.
3. Add the flour, vanilla essence and milk. Mix gently to make a stiff dough.
4. Divide the mixture into two parts and blend cocoa powder in one.
5. Thinly roll out both the halves 1/8" thick into equal sized pieces.
6. Place the chocolate piece on top of the white one. Roll the two tightly together as for swiss rolls and allow to stand in a cool place for 20-30 minutes.
7. Cut into ¼" thick slices and place on a well greased baking tray.
8. Bake in a moderate oven at 180°C/350°F for about 10-15 minutes.

» Short Crust Pastry (Basic Recipe) «

120 gm plain flour (maida)
60 gm cold fat (butter or margarine)
a pinch of salt
2 tbsp ice cold water or more - as needed

1. Sieve flour and salt in a bowl. Cut fat with a knife into small cubes.
2. Rub fat gently using finger tips until the mixture looks like fine bread crumbs. Handle the dough minimally. (Rub quickly and lightly, lifting mixture up all the time to get as much cool air in as possible.)
3. Add ice cold water. Sprinkle the water evenly over the mixture.
4. Take a palette knife or any round bladed kitchen knife and mix together lightly, cutting through and pressing together. (A knife is used to keep pastry cool. Do not use your fingers.)
5. Put down the knife and quickly bind the mixture into a smooth dough with the hand using a gentle circular motion, leaving the bowl clean.

6. Place the dough on a lightly floured board or table top and remove cracks by pressing lightly if needed.
7. Flour the rolling pin lightly. Using short sharp strokes, roll the pastry to whatever shape and size required. Roll in one direction only and turn as necessary, taking care not to stretch it. Bake as directed in individual recipes.

Note : When a recipe says 120 gm pastry, it does not mean the total weight but pastry made with 120 gm of flour.

» Cinnamon Apple Pie «

Makes 1 pie

SHORT CRUST PASTRY
180 gm flour
90 gm butter
2 tbsp ice cold water
a pinch of salt

FILLING
250 gm apples
½ cup sugar - or to taste
½ tsp lemon juice
½ tsp cinnamon (dalchini) powder

1. Make the short crust pastry as given on page 62. Roll out half into a neat round ¼" thick.

2. Put this over pie dish. The easiest way is to lift the pastry with the rolling pin. Prick with a fork. Bake blind (empty) in a moderate oven at 230°C/450°F for 15 minutes till light brown. Cool.
3. Mix all ingredients of the filling and cook together in a pan on fire till apples turn dry.
4. To make sure the bottom layer of pastry stays firm and crisp, sprinkle the baked pastry with a little flour or corn flour before adding fruit.
5. Fill with filling.
6. Roll out the second half of pastry a little larger than the size of the pie dish. Put over the top of fruit, or cut this rolled pastry into strips and make a criss-cross design on top of fruit layer.
7. Press the edges together and cut away surplus pastry. (Avoid stretching the pastry).
8. Flute or pinch the edges together.
9. Brush the top of the pie with egg white or milk, and make a fine slit or a cross in the centre for any steam to escape.
10. Bake in the centre of hot oven (425°F) for 20 minutes until the pastry is done and brown. Sprinkle with sugar, if desired.

» Jam Tarts «

Makes 6

SHORT CRUST PASTRY (DOUGH)
120 gm plain flour (maida)
60 gm fat (butter or margarine) - cold
1 tsp powdered sugar, 2 tbsp ice cold water - as needed
6 tsp jam & few roasted, salted peanuts - for filling

1. Prepare short crust pastry as given on page 62 with 120 gm flour.
2. Roll out the pastry ¼" thick. Cut into rounds using a fluted biscuit cuter of 3" diameter.
3. Clean & grease a tart tray and line with the cut rounds, making sure that they fit the mould well. Prick with a fork. Bake blind for 15 minutes in the centre of a hot oven (230°C/450°F). Take out from the oven.
4. Put 1 tsp jam in each. Sprinkle with some coarsely powdered peanuts.
5. Bake again for 5 minutes. Cool & remove jam tarts from the tray.

» Choux Pastry (Basic recipe) «

75 gm plain flour (maida)
25 gm (2 tbsp) butter or margarine
a pinch of salt
3/4 cup (140 ml) water
1 tsp sugar (optional)
2 eggs

1. Sift flour and salt together.
2. Put butter, water and sugar into a sauce pan and heat gently until butter melts; then raise the heat and rapidly bring mixture to boil.
3. Remove the pan from fire and add all the flour at once. Stir quickly with a wooden spoon until flour absorbs all liquid.
4. Return to heat and stir until a smooth ball is formed and it leaves the sides of the pan. Allow the mixture to cool a little.
5. Beat eggs till fluffy. Gradually mix eggs and beat till the eggs are well mixed. The pastry should be thick enough to hold its shape but not stiff.

» Chocolate Eclairs «

Makes 12

choux pastry made with 75 gm flour - page 67

FILLING
200 gm cream
4 tbsp powdered sugar - sifted
¼ tsp vanilla essence

CHOCOLATE GLAZE
100 gms icing sugar - sifted
2 tbsp cocoa
2-3 tbsp hot water
1 tsp melted butter

1. Make the choux pastry as given on page 67. Spoon it into a stiff (transparent) polythene bag. Cut one corner to pipe ½" thick fingers.

2. Pipe out 2" long fingers on a greased baking tray. Start piping with the cut end touching the tray and lifting it while pressing the mixture out, cut off the required length with a wet knife.
3. Place hot oven at 220°C/425°F and bake for about 20 minutes, until crisp and golden brown. (If eclairs are not thoroughly dry, reduce the heat to 180°C/350°F and continue baking for further 10 minutes).
4. Remove from the oven. Slit them down on one side to let the steam escape and leave on a wire rack to cool.
5. Beat the chilled cream & sugar till it forms soft peaks. Cool in the fridge.
6. When the eclairs are cold, fill them with whipped cream using a piping bag and a nozzle. Keep in he fridge.
7. Prepare chocolate glaze by mixing cocoa to the sifted icing sugar. Add hot water gradually and beat with a wooden spoon until smooth and glossy. Add butter. Cover the top of the filled eclairs with chocolate glaze.

Note : Add just enough water to get a pouring consistency. If glaze is not used immediately, keep it covered with a moist cloth, keeping over a bowl of hot water.

» Nut & Date Cubes «

Serves 8

½ tin milkmaid (condensed milk)
250 gms dates
½ cup oil
1 cup less 1 tbsp (85 gm) maida (plain flour)
½ cup roasted, salted groundnuts - chopped finely
½ tsp vanilla essence
1 tsp baking powder
½ tsp soda-bicarb.

Moulded Spanish Rice : Page 98

1. Remove seeds from dates and chop them finely. Soak in 5 tbsp of water with ½ tsp soda-bicarb for 4-5 hours or overnight or soak in hot water with soda for 1 hour, if you do not have so much time.
2. Sift maida with baking powder in a paraat (shallow bowl).
3. Mix dates and groundnuts gradually with the maida.
4. Beat oil and condensed milk. Add essence. Mix.
5. Add half of the maida mixture to the milk maid & oil mixture. Mix well. Add the rest of the maida. Beat well.
6. Transfer the mixture in a greased 7" x 4" loaf tin.
7. Bake in a preheated oven at 150°C/300°F for 45-50 minutes.
8. Test by inserting a knife in the highest part of the loaf. If it comes out clean, remove loaf from oven.
9. Remove the loaf from the tin after 5-7 minute
10. At serving time cut the loaf into half lengthways, and then cut into 1" slices to get cubes.

Grantinated Vegatable Lasagna : Page 41

» Malai Biscuits «

Makes 15

½ cup malai (milk topping)
½ cup sugar
½ cup maida
7-8 almonds (split into two) or 2 moti illaichi (powdered)

1. Mix malai & sugar lightly with a fork. Sift maida. Add the sifted maida to the malai mixture. Knead lightly to form a soft dough.
2. Form round balls. Flatten slightly.
3. Lightly grease an oven tray and place the balls on it, 1" apart.
4. Press almond on top or sprinkle illaichi powder on each biscuit.
5. Bake in a preheated oven at 200°C/400°F for 8-10 minutes, until edges of the biscuits are golden and the top still whitish.
6. Remove tray from the oven and quickly and carefully lift biscuits off with a knife and put them on a surface to cool and become crisp.

» Eggless Victorian Cake «

Serves 10

1 cup full (180 gm) malai (milk topping)
1½ tbsp less than 2 cups (180 gm) plain flour (maida)
1 cup (150 gm) sugar
½-3/4 cup milk - as required
1 level tsp soda-bicarb, ½ tsp baking powder
1 tsp vanilla essence

1. Sieve flour, baking powder & soda-bicarb. Keep aside.
2. Mix sugar & malai in a pan. Leave for 5-10 minutes. Mix well till sugar nearly dissolves. Do not over beat. Mix maida & essence.
3. Add enough milk as needed to obtain a dropping consistency. Beat well.
4. Pour into a preprepared 7" x 4" or 7" round tin and bake in a preheated oven at 210°C/400°F for 10 minutes. Lower the temp. to 150°C/300°F and bake for 35-40 minutes or till the cake is done.

» Madeleines «

(small cakes)

Makes 16-18

100 gm (1 cup) flour (maida)
4 eggs
100 gm (3/4 cup) powdered sugar
100 gm salted butter or table margarine - melted
1 tsp vanilla essence
2 tbsp strawberry or mixed fruit jam - heated
½ cup dessicated coconut
glace cherries and almonds (toasted) - to decorate

1. Sift flour. Melt butter on low flame & keep aside.
2. Boil a small pan half filled with water. Remove from fire.
3. Break the eggs in a larger pan which can rest on top of the smaller pan.
4. Add sugar to the eggs and beat sugar & eggs with an electric beater till 4 times in volume. The mixture becomes thick, pale in colour & attains a dropping consistency. Add essence.
5. Remove the pan from the hot water. Add melted butter gradually mixing in very lightly.
6. Fold in a little of the flour (2-3 tbsp) at one time. Fold in all the flour gradually.
7. Fill three-quarters full greased small cake moulds with mixture.
8. Bake in a moderately hot oven, 400°F/200°C for 10-15 minutes. Turn out on to a wire tray to cool.
9. Mix jam with 1-2 tbsp water & heat on very low flame till jam melts.
10. When cold brush each madeleine with jam and roll in dessicated coconut.
11. Decorate top of each with half a glace cherry and toasted almonds.

» Peanut Macaroons «

Makes 8 biscuits

1 egg white
a pinch of salt
few drops almond essence
1/3 cup powdered sugar
2/3 cup salted, roasted, peanuts - ground coarsely

1. Beat the egg white with a pinch of salt in a clean dry bowl, until very stiff peaks can be formed when the beater is lifted. Add the almond essence.
2. Fold in sugar and ground peanuts gently. If the egg white is exceptionally large then add a little more ground nuts. The mixture should be of a dropping consistency.
3. Spoon the mixture into round heaps, 1" apart, on a well greased baking tray. Bake for 15-20 minutes in the centre of a moderate oven, 350°F/180°C. When nearly cold, remove from the tray with a sharp flat spoon.

» Coconut Macaroons «

Makes 8 biscuits

1 egg white
a pinch of salt
1 cup desiccated coconut
½ cup powdered sugar

1. Beat the egg white with a pinch of salt in a clean dry bowl, until very stiff peaks can be formed when the beater is lifted.
2. Fold in sugar and dessicated coconut gently. If the egg white is exceptionally large then add a little more coconut. The mixture should be of a dropping consistency.
3. Spoon the mixture into round heaps, 1" apart, on a well greased baking tray. Bake for 15-20 minutes in the centre of a moderate oven, 350°F/180°C. Remove from the oven.
4. When nearly cold, remove from the tray with a sharp flat spoon.

›› Cashewnut Cookies ‹‹

100 gm (1 cup) maida (plain flour)
2 to 3 tbsp finely chopped cashewnuts
75 gm (½ cup) butter, margarine or vanaspati ghee
50 grams (1/3 cup) powdered sugar
2 to 3 drops almond essence or 1 tsp vanilla essence

1. Sieve the flour.
2. Preheat oven at 200C/400°F.
3. Beat butter & sugar very well until light & creamy.
4. Add the essence and beat again.
5. Add the flour and mix gently to form a soft dough.
6. Form into small balls and roll into the chopped cashewnuts.
7. Arrange on a greased tray, keeping 1" apart.
8. Bake in a preheated oven for 15 to 20 minutes.
9. Remove from the tray when slightly cold.

Savoury TEA-TIME Eats

» Savoury Mushroom Loaf «

Picture on page 54

Serves 6

100 gms (1cup) maida
2 big potatoes - boiled & grated (1½ cups potato paste)
1 tsp salt, ¼ tsp baking powder
2 semi heaped tbsp vanaspati ghee or margarine - (¼ cup melted)
(do not use oil)

FILLING
3 tbsp oil
2 laung (cloves) - crushed
2 onions - chopped finely
½ packet (100 gms) mushrooms - sliced
1 tomato - chopped finely
1 green chilli - deseeded & chopped finely
salt & pepper to taste

1. Mix grated, boiled potato with maida in a paraat. Add salt & baking pd.
2. Melt ghee or margarine & pour over the maida. Mix well to form a firm dough. Add enough ghee to form a dough. Knead well. Chill in the fridge
3. To prepare the filling, heat oil. Add onions. Cook till transparent.
4. Add mushroom slices and stir fry for 4-5 min. on medium flame till brown & well cooked. Add laung & tomato. Cook for 2-3 min. Add green chilli. Add salt & pepper to taste. Cook till almost dry. Cool filling.
5. To prepare the loaf, grease a flat baking tray generously.
6. Make 2 balls with the cold potato dough. Roll out one ball into a rectangular chappati, ¼" thick. Trim the sides neatly with a knife.
7. Place on a greased tray. Sprinkle a little maida. Spread the filling.
8. Mix trimmings with the second ball & roll out a bigger rectangle. Trim sides. Place it on the filling so as to cover the sides. Join the edges to form a loaf. Pinch edges. Brush with milk or egg mixed with a little water. Make slits ½" apart. Roll out the left over trimmings & cut petals. Make a flower.
9. Bake in a heated oven at 170°C/325°F for 30-40 min, keeping the tray on the upper shelf because the loaf tends to turn brown faster at the bottom.

» Special Crusty Pizza «

Makes 3

PIZZA BASE
¼ cup lukewarm water
½ tsp sugar
2 tsp heaped dried yeast (10 gms)
1 cup milk
1½ tbsp oil
1 tsp salt, 1 tbsp sugar
3 cups (300 gm) flour (maida)

PIZZA SAUCE
4 tomatoes
1 tbsp oil
¼ tsp ajwain (carom seeds)
5-6 flakes garlic - crushed

3 tbsp tomato ketchup
1 tsp chilli sauce or ½ tsp chilli powder
salt & pepper to taste

PIZZA TOPPING
1 capsicum - chopped
1 onion - chopped
200 gm pizza cheese
salt & pepper to taste

1. To prepare the pizza base, mix warm water and sugar. Add yeast. Shake the cup gently to mix the yeast. Cover it and leave it in a warm place till the granules disappear and it becomes frothy. (10-15 minutes)
2. Mix milk, oil, salt and sugar in a pan. Keep aside.
3. When the yeast becomes frothy, heat this milk mixture to make it lukewarm. Add the ready yeast mix to the like warm milk mixture.
4. Add this yeast and milk mixture to the maida and knead well to make a smooth dough.

5. Grease a polythene, brush the dough with oil and put it in the polythene. Keep covered in a warm place to swell for 1 hour till it doubles in size.
6. Now punch it down to it's original size, brush with oil and keep it back in the polythene for another 15 min in a warm place or till it swells again.
7. Make 3 balls and roll each into ¼" thickness for pizza base. Prick each base with a fork. Bake in a preheated oven at 200°C for 10-15 minutes.
8. To prepare the pizza sauce, blend tomatoes to a puree in a mixer.
9. Heat oil. Add ¼ tsp ajwain. Stir fry for 1 minute. Add garlic. Stir fry for ½ minute. Add tomato puree, tomato ketchup, chilli sauce, salt & pepper. Cook till thick.
10. To prepare the pizza, spread 2 tbsp of pizza sauce on the pizza base, leaving the edges.
11. Add salt & pepper to capsicum & onion. Sprinkle some on the base over the sauce. Grate cheese directly over the onion-capsicum mixture.
12. Grill by keeping the pizza directly on the perforated plate or wire rack of a hot oven for about 5 minutes till the base of the pizza becomes crisp and the cheese melts. Serve hot.

» Cheese Straws «

100 gm flour (maida)
pinch salt
pinch of white pepper
50 gm butter - beaten well to make it smooth
50 gm cheese - finely grated
1 egg yolk
1 tbsp water

1. Sieve the flour, salt and pepper.
2. Rub in the butter with your finger tips, lifting the hand high above the flour while mixing the butter, until mixture resembles fine bread crumbs.
3. Stir in the cheese and bind together with the egg yolk and water. Form into a firm dough. Roll out the dough and cut into thin fingers ¼" wide.
4. Twist the fingers and place on a greased baking tray.
5. Bake in a hot oven at 425°F/220°C for 7-10 minutes.
6. Remove from the tray after cooling.

» Paneer Potato Ring «

Serves 4

DOUGH
5 heaped tbsp of boiled, mashed & chilled potato paste (2 boiled potatoes)
5 semi heaped tbsp of maida
5 tbsp melted vanaspati ghee or margarine
½ tsp salt or to taste, ¼ tsp black pepper, ¼ tsp red chilli powder

FILLING
½ onion - chopped finely
1 green chilli - chopped finely
50 gms paneer (cottage cheese) - mashed roughly
½ tsp saunf (aniseeds) optional
1 tbsp oil
¼ tsp haldi (turmeric pd), ¼ tsp chilli powder
salt to taste

1. To prepare the dough mix all the ingredients. Do not add water. Chill the dough in the dridge for some time.
2. To prepare the filling, heat oil. Add onion and green chillies. Cook till onion turns transparent. Add saunf. Add haldi & chilli powder.
3. Add paneer & cook for 1-2 minutes. Cool the filling.
4. Make a ball of the chilled potato dough. Keep the ball on a greased baking tray. Flatten it to ¼" thickness & spread it to from a 7" long and 3" broad rectange approx.
5. Place the filling length-wise in the centre.
6. Lift the sides, overlapping each other to make a roll.
7. Turns the edges of the roll to form a ring. Join the edges with some water.
8. Brush with beaten egg or milk. Sprinkle some ajwain. Make slits 2" apart.
9. Bake in a hot oven at 200°C for half an hour till golden brown.
10. To serve, cut into pieces at the slits.

Note : It is important to use margarine or ghee like rath or dalda. Oil must not be substituted for ghee.

» Pleated Bread «

Serves 6

FILLING
1 onion - finely chopped
3 tbsp butter
1½ cups mushrooms - chopped
½ cup peas - boiled
1 small potato - boiled and mashed
salt and pepper to taste
1 tsp tomato ketchup

DOUGH
2 cups flour (maida)
1 tsp baking powder
½ tsp salt
½ cup butter - cold
½ cup milk

1. Heat the butter and fry the onion until golden. Add the chopped mushrooms. Cook till done. Add peas and mashed potatoes. Mix well & cook for 3-4 minutes. Add salt & pepper to taste. Mix tomato ketchup and remove from fire. Cool the filling.
2. For the bread, sieve the flour, baking powder and salt into a paraat.
3. Cut butter into small cubes. Rub the butter into the flour with your finger tips till it resembles fine bread crumbs.
4. Add the milk gradually to form a soft dough.
5. Roll out the dough to a rectangular shape, about 9" x 12" Mark lengthwise into 3 equal parts (but do not cut).
6. Cut the outer parts diagonally, into small, equal strips, ½" broad. Place the prepared filling in the centre, lengthwise.
7. Lift the strips from the 2 sides alternately and lay them on top of the filling. Brush with milk or egg.
8. Bake in a moderate oven at 180°C/350°F for 30 to 40 minutes, until the top is well browned. Serve hot with tomato sauce.

» Cheese on Toast «

Serves 2

2 slices bread - toasted
1 cube (25 gm) cheese or 2 slices cheese
tomato slices & coriander to garnish
Butter - enough to spread
salt & freshly ground pepper to taste

1. Toast slices till crisp.
2. Butter them.
3. Grate cheese from the fine side of the grater directly on the toast.
4. Arrange 2 tomato slices & 2 coriander leaves.
5. Sprinkle salt & freshly ground pepper.
6. Put under a grill for 2 minutes. Cut into two halves & serve.

BAKED RICE
ROTIS & BREAD ROLLS

» Crispy Baked Biryani «

Serves 4

RICE
1 cup uncooked rice
1 tej patta (bay leaf)
1 tsp salt, 1 tsp oil
juice of ½ a lemon
6 cups water

OTHER INGREDIENTS
3 slices bread - cut into tiny cubes & fried
3/4 cup shelled peas, 2 carrots - cut into tiny cubes

MASALA
3 tbsp oil
2 onions, 2 tomatoes
¼ tsp haldi (turmeric) powder

¼ tsp red chilli powder, 1 tsp salt
2 chhoti illaichi (green cardamom) - powdered
¼ cup fresh malai - (optional), ¼ cup fresh curd - well beaten

1. Wash, clean & soak rice. Boil water with salt, oil, tej patta & lemon juice.
2. Drain rice & add to the boiling water. Stir. Boil rice till done. Strain.
3. Cut bread into tiny cubes (as for soups) & deep fry to a golden colour.
4. Boil carrots & peas with ¼ tsp salt till soft. Strain. Keep aside.
5. To prepare masala, grind onions & tomatoes to a paste together.
6. Heat oil. Add onion - tomato paste & stir fry till dry & oil separates.
7. Add haldi, red chilli & salt. Cook for 2 minutes.
8. Mix the malai with well beaten curd & add to the masala. Cook for 3-4 minutes. Add powdered seeds of 2 chhoti illaichi. Mix.
9. Add the strained vegetables. Mix for 1 minute. Keep aside.
10. Just before serving, add the bread cubes. Mix well.
11. Mix the rice gently, but nicely. Put in an oven proof ceramic handi or dish. Cover with foil. Bake for 10 minutes in a moderately hot oven till the rice gets hot. Serve.

» Bread Rolls «

Makes 16

450 gm (4½ cups) flour (maida)
2 tsp salt
5 gm (1½ tsp) yeast
1 tsp sugar
30 gm (2 tbsp) salted butter
13/4 cup (300 ml) water

1. Mix ¼ cup warm water with ½ tsp sugar. Dissolve yeast in it. Cover & keep aside in a warm place for 10 minutes to make it frothy.
2. Mix remaining sugar & salt in remaining water.
3. Sieve flour. Combine flour with above mixture. Add the yeast mix.
4. Knead to a smooth soft dough.

5. Beat butter till creamy. Mix the whipped butter into the dough & knead well. Keep aside in a warm place for 1 hour.
6. Punch the dough & keep aside for 45 minute.
7. Divide into 16 portions. Shape them into long rolls between your hands.
8. Tie the two ends of the roll to get a knotted roll.
9. Place on a greased tray covered with a wet cloth for sometime.
10. Bake in a preheated oven at 450°F for 10-15 minutes.

» Moulded Spanish Rice «

Picture on page 71

Serves 6

1 cup basmati rice
7-8 fresh beans - cut into small diagonal pieces
1 carrot - cut into tiny cubes, 1 capsicum - cut into tiny pieces
1 onion - finely chopped, 2 tomatoes - finely chopped
1 tbsp curd, 4 tbsp oil
1 tsp garam masala, 1½ tsp salt or to taste
6-7 flakes garlic, 2-3 red chillies whole

POWDER TOGETHER
2 sticks dalchini (cinnamon), 3-4 laung (cloves)
3-4 saboot kali mirch (pepper corns)

GARNISHING
1 firm tomato - cut into slices
a few lettuce leaves - dipped in ice cold water for 30 min. or more

1. Boil rice in plenty of water till just tender. Do not over cook. Strain. Keep aside.
2. Wash beans & carrots. Put in a pressure cooker with 3-4 tbsp water. Keep on fire. As soon as the hissing sound starts, remove from fire. Do not let the whistle come. Keep aside.
3. Powder the whole spices together coarsely on a chakla-belan.
4. Crush garlic & whole red chillies together on the chakla-belan.
5. Heat oil. Add onions. Cook till light brown. Add garlic-chilli paste. Cook for 1-2 minutes.
6. Add curd, tomatoes & capsicum. Cook on low heat for 1 minutes. Add the powdered saboot masala, steamed carrots-beans & boiled rice. Add salt & garam masala. Stir fry for 2-3 minutes.
7. Wash (rinse) a jelly or a cake mould. Do not wipe it. Grease it with oil.
8. Arrange tomato slices on the sides of the greased jelly mould. Pack with the ready rice. Cover with a foil. At serving time put in a preheated hot oven for 10 minutes. Unmould on to a plate lined with lettuce leaves or decorate the plate with fresh coriander with stalks & lemon twists.

» Tandoori Parantha «

Serves 4

2½ cups atta (wheat flour)
1 cup water (approx.)
½ tsp salt
2-3 tbsp ghee

1. Keep ghee in the fridge for some time, so that it solidifies.
2. Make a soft dough with atta, salt and water. Keep aside for half an hour.
3. Divide the dough into 6 equal balls. Flatten each ball, roll out each into a round of 5" diameter.
4. Spread 1 tsp of solidified ghee.
5. Make a slit, starting from the centre till any one end.
6. Start rolling from the slit, to form an even cone. Roll out, to a diameter of 5", applying pressure only at the centre.
7. Place on a baking tray and cook in a preheated oven at 240°C/475°F for 4-5 minutes till cooked. Do not over bake.
8. Remove from the oven and holding the parantha in between a chimta (tongs), make it brown on the gas directly.
9. Spread butter & serve hot.

Note : It is important to put the paranthas in a very **hot oven**. Preheat the oven to the maximum temperature.

For a large gathering, you may bake the paranthas in the oven & keep them in a casserole. Brown them on the gas at serving time.

» Mexican Rice Casserole «

Serves 4

RICE
1 cup uncooked rice
1 tsp salt
1 tsp oil
2 laung (cloves)
6 cups water

MEXICAN SAUCE
4-6 flakes garlic - chopped & crushed
2 dried red whole chillies - broken into bits
2 onions - chopped very finely
1 big tomato - chopped very finely
1 tbsp tomato sauce
½ - ¾ tsp salt (to taste)

OTHER INGREDIENTS
2-3 brinjals (long small variety)
1 tsp salt
½ tsp red chilli pd.
2 tbsp besan (gram flour)
oil to fry
25-50 gm cheese - grated (vijaya or mozzarella)
1 tbsp butter - melted.

1. Wash clean & soak rice. Boil water with salt, laung & oil.
2. Drain rice & add to the boiling water. Stir. Cook till rice is done. Strain. Keep boiled rice aside.
3. Wash & cut brinjals into ¼" thick slices. Spread on a plate & sprinkle salt & chilli powder. Rub well. Keep aside for 10 minutes, so that they leave water.
4. To prepare the sauce, heat oil. Make the flame low. Add crushed garlic & broken red chilli bits. Cook for 1 minute.
5. Add onions & cook till they turn light brown.

6. Add tomatoes & cook for 4-5 minutes, till tomatoes turn soft & pulpy.
7. Add the tomato sauce & salt. Mix & remove from fire. Keep aside.
8. Sprinkle 2 tbsp besan on the brinjals. Rub the besan so as to coat the brinjals.
9. Deep fry the brinjals to a golden brown colour.
10. To assemble the casserole, grease a 2" high borosil dish with butter & spread rice in it.
11. Melt butter in a small pan on low flame & pour over the rice.
12. Cover the rice with a single layer of fried brinjals.
13. Spread the Mexican sauce over the brinjals. Press lightly with a spoon.
14. Grate cheese generously on the sauce. Keep aside.
15. At serving time, put in a preheated oven at 180°C & bake till rice turns hot.